The

# Rambling Mind

## Laura Licker

PublishAmerica
Baltimore

Hardcover 978-1-4512-1179-5
Softcover 978-1-4489-5501-5
PUBLISHED BY PUBLISHAMERICA, LLLP
www.publishamerica.com
Baltimore

Printed in the United States of America

Dedicated to the ones who mean the most to me. Mama and Daddy, Sy and Brandy, Alan and Debbie, Buck and Joy, Aaron, Sarah, Tim and Seth. You all have touched my heart in many different ways. I am a better person for having you in my life. You all are very important and mean the world to me. I have much love for all of you.

# Table of Contents

Is It To Be ................................................................8
Would It Be Different .............................................10
Ghosts ...................................................................11
All Your Own .........................................................12
People That You Meet ............................................14
Smile .....................................................................16
When Do You Worry ...............................................17
Has It Ever Occured To You ....................................20
His Importance To Me ............................................22
When Do You Know ................................................23
Who Is There .........................................................24
Looking For Him ....................................................25
Gorgeous ...............................................................26
What Is Going On In Your Head ...............................27
How Does It Feel ...................................................30
My Chica ...............................................................32
Calling Of The Waves ............................................34
Learn From The Field .............................................36
Something Is Wrong ...............................................37
Love For Someone You Never Met ...........................39
She Is My Sister ....................................................40
Finally Happy .........................................................41
The Beauty Of Nature .............................................42
She Has Been Adopted ...........................................43
Always So Worried ..................................................44
The Place I Call Home ............................................45
She Is Missed ........................................................46
Will We Be The Death Of Ourselves .........................48
What Judgment Are You Guilty Of............................50
Over The Edge .......................................................52
Let The Fire Burn ...................................................53

What Is The Next Step ........................................................ 54
Yoga With A friend ........................................................... 56
To See Her In Pain ............................................................ 57
Does It Really Matter ........................................................ 58
Make The Pain Stop .......................................................... 59
Is This The Day You Die .................................................... 60
Gone But Not Forgotten .................................................... 61
And So It Goes ................................................................. 62
Just To Drive .................................................................... 63
Our Country's Hero ........................................................... 64
Are Birds Crazy ................................................................ 65
Pain In His Head ............................................................... 66
The Miracle Of Life .......................................................... 67
His Eyes Say It ................................................................. 68
Expressions In Sleep ......................................................... 69
Late Night Run ................................................................. 70
To Bleed ........................................................................... 73
Silently Screaming ............................................................ 75

# Silence

In silence you sit there. You hear nothing. No TV, no music, nothing turned on. You do not hear the motor on the fridge. You do not hear the circling of the fan above you. They are just white noise, not noticeable. All you hear is silence. It fills your ears and fills your head. You have no conscience thought on your mind. No worries, no cares, just nothingness. The silence builds, higher and higher, louder and louder. It fills your body like it fills your head. You feel it as it ever so slowly over takes all of you. It controls you. It consumes you. No where to run, no escaping the maddening silence. Slowly it eats away at everything as you know it to be, until the silence is all that you know, all that you have left. Who will come and take it all away? Who will break and destroy the maddening silence? Who will be your everlasting sound? Who will rescue you from the death of silence?

# Is It To Be

I walk into the place and find a seat where I can be comfy.
The music is playing and people are enjoying themselves all
around. As I look around I see him. Something about him
mesmerizes me and I can not look away. He spots me watching
him and watches me back. We make no changes in our
expressions, just our eyes lock together. When the music
finishes playing and it is time to go…he walks over to me. Still
our faces remain neutral and nothing is said. As he stands
there, he holds out his hand to me. I reach up and place my
hand in his and he wraps his fingers around mine as I stand up.
He leads me out of the building and into his car. My eyes
never leave him. We ride a short distance and then he helps
me out. As he takes my hand again we walk into the place that
I instinctively know as his home. He leads me into the bedroom
and ever so slowly we come together and make beautiful
passionate love like we never have before. As we lie there in

the aftermath, he wraps his arms around me and softly

whispers, "Never leave me, I am broken without you". I close

my eyes and whisper back, "Never"… then we sleep…

# Would It Be Different

Would life be something else if it was not so hard at times?
Is it just a bunch of challenges to work through on a regular
basis? Of course it has to have its moments of fun and
entertainment thrown in to break things up. Is it all some kind
of test to see what we can handle? Do we all have a purpose for
being here in the first place? And if we do…how is it decided
who gets what purpose? And are some more important than
others? Or are they all equal in their own way? And are we
suppose to know our purpose or are we just judged for it when
our time is through? Is it even possible that there are any
answers to these questions? The bottom line I believe is that
life is one big mystery.

# Ghosts

Do you believe in ghosts?

Have you ever felt a hand touch your back when you know that you are home alone? Have you ever felt someone sit or lay down next to you when you are by yourself? Have you ever felt any kind of presents of someone being with you?

I believe in ghosts.

# All Your Own

You feel the pressure of the day closing in on you. Your head is pounding so hard you think it might explode and you hope it does just to get some relief. Your heart beats faster and faster. Your chest hurts from all the pressure and you can clearly see it move with each beat. You start to sweat and you feel clammy at the same time. It feels like every nerve ending in your body is exposed. You scream but nobody hears you. You cry but all that does is make you hurt more. You can not leave and break away, you have a responsibility to get things done. What can you do, where can you go? You need it all to go away. To stop the hurting. To take this terrible pain away. You want to live but you feel you will die at any moment. You want to run and leave it all behind. You just do not want to hurt anymore. Make it stop fast, right now. How will you survive to get through another day… some how you must. There are things you can not leave behind. People who need you and count on you.

Will they be there for you? All you have is trust to go

on. Trust the ones you care about and have faith in them to be

there and to see you through all that life brings you…… as you

will always be there for them simply because you care and you

value them as who they are…… and you would be lost without

them. They are your world and forever will be.

# People That You Meet

I get up in the morning and when I leave the house I get in

my truck to go for a drive. I have no place in particular to go. I

just drive. I see other people driving and walking on the

sidewalks. I wonder who they are and what kind of person are

they? I drive to a park since it's a beautiful day. Then I walk

on the path that surrounds it. Lots of people here today. I

smile and say hi to each one that I pass. Someone stops me and

asks for the time. I answer them and they seem reluctant to

walk away. I'm curious as to why. We stand there watching each

other. Then they make an unsure face and walk away. I decide

that's enough of the park and I drive to the mall. I wander in

and out of stores. Looking at different things but not really

seeing them. Again I smile and say hi to people I pass. Just

being friendly to all that cross my path. I see all different

people and not know who they are. But I wonder if they will ever

play a part in my life. I get a sense that I am being watched. I look around trying not to be noticed. Too late, he walks toward me. I have a moment of panic. Unsure what to do. Should I bolt or walk into the nearest store or stand my ground? I stay rooted to the spot I am in. Unable to do anything. Will he be friendly and kind or will he be my enemy? Will he cause me more pain in my life or will he be my destiny? Will he fill the void I have inside me and give me back what is missing or will he be the death of me? I am fearful and panicked but I am also curious and hopeful. He walks closer and closer still. Now he stands tall in front of me. I look into his eyes and try to read the kind of person he is. I wonder, could he be? He reaches out his hand to me and I raise mine to take a hold…

Then I wake up.

# Smile

Do not be afraid to smile,

you never know who is

falling in love with it!

# When Do You Worry

You are going through your day like any other day. It is a

Saturday so you decide to do some chores around the house.

Just regular things like cleaning and laundry that always seem

to need to be done. Then all of a sudden you get a sharp pain in

your belly and it makes you double over. You wince in pain and

you quickly go through everything you have done recently in

your mind. Trying to figure out what could of caused this pain.

Then the pain subsides and you go back to what you were doing

and you never do put a reason to it. You finally finish your day

and climb into bed. While you lie there you wonder what that

pain was all about but soon let it go and fall asleep. The next

day comes and as you are going about your business, the same

pain comes again. Still you do not know why. This day it comes

more than once but you do not know what to do about it.

Before you know it the days go by and turn into a week. The

pain seems to be maybe increasing in frequency. That is when you discover something else start to happen. You look in disbelief and there it is…blood. You feel a bit of panic start. How can this be happening? What can possibly be going on? More time goes by and then you notice something in the blood. You stand there staring at it… could that be what is inside me? After being stubborn for this amount of time and with all the pain coming and going whenever it pleases… now you know without a doubt. You can not put it off any longer. Time to see a doctor… have to find out what this is. So you go and they tell you that your insides are in a very bad way. They want to do tests and exams…. have to be exact. So they do. And they tell you that your digestive tract is full of ulcers. They must try to control it with medicine… hopefully they can. They do not know what causes it but it seems to be common. If it can not be controlled then they will have to remove that part of your insides. You are all alone to deal with this. No one is there to fight for you, to give you support. Who do you cry to? Who do you voice your fears to? What will happen? Is it a life with taking pills every day or will it even make any difference? Will you still lose your insides no matter what? Then it hits you... why is this even happening? What is the purpose of all this? There must be a reason for it... but what? So then you are determined to go through whatever it takes to take care of this. You must not give up on yourself. You have a purpose and reason for being here. All this just plays a small part in it. You will overcome this moment in your life. You will succeed and beat this. This is your test to be true to yourself. To make a difference in life and to others. You do have value. You are a worthy person.

# Has It Ever Occured To You

Has it ever occurred to you to say hi to the random people

that you walk by?

Has it ever occurred to you to wave hello to the random people

that you drive by?

Has it ever occurred to you to call someone out of the blue

that you have not talked to in a long time to see how they are doing?

Has it ever occurred to you to leave some sort of message for

someone, whether you know them well or not, just to let them

know they were thought of?

Has it ever occurred to you to really listen when someone talks

to you?

Has it ever occurred to you to lend your support to someone

in need?

Has it ever occurred to you to offer comfort to those you say

you care about?

Has it ever occurred to you that you are needed?

Whether you really know someone or not, let them know they are valued. Spread the joy a smile can bring. Take the time to brighten someone's day. Everyone needs to know they matter in this life. Take the time to care…. really care.

# His Importance To Me

When we first started talking, I thought he was interesting. The more I learned about him, the more I wanted to know. My anticipation to spend time with him grew every day, even if it was just to talk. It only takes the thought of him to bring a smile to my face. As our friendship grew stronger, so did the importance of him being in my life. When he is far away, my heart aches for him, like a piece of me is missing. I am truly blessed to have him in my life. Without him being there, I would be forever lost. He is a gift, that I treasure for life.

# When Do You Know

When do you know it is time to give up everything you know

as it is?

When do you know it is time to move on and start again?

When do you know it is time to shut the door to the past as

you know it and open another door to a new future?

When do you stop being so scared and hopeful for life as you

know it and take a giant leap of faith into an uncertain future?

When do you say good bye to the life you have known for half

your life?

When do you start again?

# Who Is There

Who is there when you scream out into the darkness?

Who is there when you cry out in pain?

Who is there when you reach for a guiding hand?

Who is there when you need comfort?

Who is there when you need to be reassured?

Who is there to help you with your fears?

Who is there to share your sorrow?

Who is there to laugh with?

Who is there to experience new things with?

Who is there to go to new places with?

Who is there to take away the loneliness?

Who is there to share your life with?

Who is there to give and receive love to?

Is there someone there or are you forever alone..........

# Looking For Him

Him

He means everything to me. He is my love and my life. It would be my joy to try to take care of him and keep him comfy. He is always there for me no matter what. Always ready to listen and help in any way he can. He gives me lots of love like no one else, something I have never had before. He shows me what it is like to be truly cared about and I want to do the same for him.

Miss him

I miss him when he is not with me. I wait for him to return to me. I am lost without him.

Need him

A very important part of me is what he is. I am incomplete without him. I need him forever in my life. I give my love to him.

# Gorgeous

Someone who has a beautiful mind, soul and heart.

Someone who is kind, caring and understanding.

Someone who is respectful and honest.

Someone who cares about you, no matter what.

Someone who is there for you in your time of need which

includes your happiness and your sorrow.

Someone who is a true person and not a phony.

Someone who you are honored to call your friend.

This is what a gorgeous person is…

Are you one?

# What Is Going On In Your Head

It is 3 am and you are lying in bed staring up at the ceiling

and watching the fan go round and round. Everything is going on

in your head but at the same time there is nothing inside. You

sling back the covers and slowly sit up, you hang your head and

just sit a moment. Then you get up and pull a shirt on over your

head and pull on some jeans. You then jam your feet into some

shoes and walk through the dark house to the front door.

Slowly your hand reaches to open the door and you walk out

never giving it a second thought. You just start walking with no

place to go. Out of your yard, down your street. You keep going,

can not stop, who knows where you will end up. After walking

around aimlessly you find yourself on a bridge and you suddenly

stop and look around. You think to yourself, how did I get here?

Have I ever seen this place before? All you know is it is calling

to you. You can not leave. There is a power that is stronger

than you. You walk over to the edge and look down. The water mesmerizes you. You stand there and just stare. It looks so peaceful. There is no pain there, no worries, no feelings. Just a relaxing place to lose yourself in. You keep staring at it. You try to empty your mind and just see the water. Then you wonder, what is on the bottom? Is it soft and sandy or hard with rocks? Would it hurt to go in or would you feel nothing? Would you suffer under water or would you immediately go to another place? Then it hits you, would someone find you if you went in or would you just be gone? Would anyone notice you missing, would they even care? Would they mourn you or would they celebrate you being gone? You do not know any of these answers, you stopped believing in trust and faith. You have been hurt so many times, it is all you expect now. You want all the pain to stop. You have been hurting for so long it is all you know. You think to yourself, why go on? It does not even matter. You believe you have no meaning to anyone or anything. Nothing makes a difference. Life will go on, the same as always. You look at the water again and you see the current moving it along.

You look up above you and whisper "Forgive me". Then you close

your eyes and step off of the bridge…

# How Does It Feel

You haven't talked to her in a few years, because you cut her out of your life and put a major wall between you. Living as her child has always been painful for you because no matter what you ever did, it was never good enough for her. You always felt like you didn't belong in the family because you were always the different one. How do you grow up in life and turn out to be the complete opposite of her? You see it as a good thing the way you turned out but in the end, she sees it as her failure that she didn't teach you the right things. So anyway, now here it is, years later and you try again to have her in your life. So you are more nervous than a person can imagine. You are so scared about what will happen when you pick up the phone. Then you bite the bullet and call her. For the most part, it goes well but she still lets it be known that you have made mistakes and she didn't teach you something right in life some how. They tell you to accept her as she is, but for you, they will make sure you are always aware of your mistakes and it is not acceptable

to them. All you ever wanted was to be accepted by her, and

along with the rest of the family, but apparently it doesn't

work that way. Oh well, what can you do right? It's just the way

it is. The bottom line is, she's your mother and that means

something to you. Good or bad, you care about her and you

want that connection with her, so you just take it as it comes.

# My Chica

She is the one thing I believe I did right in my life. I tried the best I could to teach her right from wrong, I am well aware that I have made mistakes along the way. After all, I didn't have an instruction book with directions. She means the world to me and she is my pride and joy. I have always done what I could to be there for her and in her corner no matter what, and that will never change. I am severely protective of her, sometimes maybe too much, who knows for sure? She and I are very close to each other, always have been and hopefully always will be. Heaven help anyone who ever causes her pain in life. Maybe I have failed in not teaching her to be more independent and her lack of a strong work ethic, but then again those are minor compared to other things she could be or have against her. After all she's not a criminal or abusive or destructive. She's a good person, who cares about others. Her manners are there, when she chooses to use them, but don't most people? My chica is shy for the most part and very passive. When something bothers her, she clams up until she decides she's ready to face it. When she's mad, you know it, even with her being quiet. Bottom line is, she is my angel sent from above. My life since day one, is what she has always been. She will forever be my one and only chica. I am filled with a never ending love for her, always have been and always will be.

# Calling Of The Waves

It is the middle of the night. Everyone is asleep except for you. Quietly you get up and get dressed. Something is calling to you but you are not sure what it is. You slip on your shoes and grab your coat. The next thing you do is walk out the door. You start walking, not sure where you are going. Something tells you which way to go, but you do not know what it is. You keep walking, block after block. Then you hear it. The sound your ears have been waiting for. You see the ocean ahead of you. You walk through the sand of the beach. You keep walking until you get to the waters edge. You sit down on the cold sand and snuggle in deeper inside your coat, for the winter temperature is biting at you. You watch the waves and slowly you are mesmerized by them. You know they are so powerful and yet so calming at the same time. You start to wonder what it would feel like to be in the water. Would the coldness cause you pain or would you instantly go numb all the way through to your bones? Would you be able to move around or would you drown due to shock? Would you float or would you sink? You hear nothing but the waves. It gets harder to resist. The need to know these answers keeps getting stronger and stronger. Slowly you stand up. You walk forward and the water laps at your feet. You keep walking. You do not feel the cold and you do not feel the water. Soon the water is up to your waist. You keep going farther in. Then up to your shoulders. You still can not stop. The water is all you know. It is all you see, it is all you hear. The water owns your soul and it wants your body. Your head then submerges into the water and you are forever consumed by the waves.

# Learn From The Field

Have you ever slowly walked through a field and heard the

whisper of the grass as it brushes by you?

Have you ever laid down in a field and watched the clouds roll

by?

Have you ever closed your eyes in a field and breathed in the

smell of the grass and earth surrounding you?

Have you ever stood in a field and listened to the small

creatures, such as birds, frogs and even bugs?

Have you ever been in a field and played nature's

instrument, such as whistling through a piece of grass?

You can learn a lot from one little area called a field. All you

have to do is take the time to look, listen, hear and smell. It

is a beautiful way to spend the day.

# Something Is Wrong

You go to bed that night thinking everything is fine.

Suddenly you are woken up. Out of your groggy state of being,

you realize it is your phone that wakes you up. You answer it

and hear panic and aggravation on the other end. Someone

you love is lost from where they need to go. They need your

help to get them to the right place. They have taken too

many wrong turns. You can not help them because neither of

you is sure where they are. They seem to have gone in

endless circles. You finally hang up unable to help at all. You

feel useless and like you have let them down. Now you can

not go back to sleep. You lay in your bed and stare at the

ceiling. Hour after hour you look at your clock wondering if

they are alright. You keep getting up and look to see if their

car is home yet. All you see is an empty space. As the minutes

tick by, all you can do is wait. An emergency sent them out

late into the night. Now all you want to do is know that the ones you love are safe. Hours later you finally crash with

exhaustion, no longer able to keep your eyes open. Sometime

the next day is when you find out everything is ok.

# Love For Someone You Never Met

I felt the changes coming on. Little by little things were different. I knew there was new life from deep within. Instantly there was love so strong for this new being inside of me. I felt so special to be a creator. I could not wait to be able to know this little one. I wanted a long life together to learn new things.

But this was not to be. This life was taken from me. Soon after it started it was gone. All I had left was an empty space. I lost the one I had so much love for. Where was this love to go?

# She Is My Sister

She has been my sister in law for many years. But to me that is not how I see her. I have learned very much from her after all this time. I am grateful to have her in my life, for she means so much to me. She has guided me through a stressful subject, for without her I would be lost. I see her as a very knowledgeable person. Over the years she has given me so much. To have her kindness and caring mean everything to me. I do not call her my sister in law. She is much more important than that. She is and forever will be my sister.

# Finally Happy

For as long as I can remember there has always been depression. So much sadness I never knew what to do. My whole life it was always the same. So many times I would cry and cry for no reason at all. I always wanted things to be different. Growing up there was too much anger in the home. Once I became an adult I had things that made me happy. But I was never happy in general. Over the years I have had things to work through in my life and in my head. I believe I have now risen out of the ashes of sorrow. Now so many years in my life have passed but I can finally say I am truly happy and I love my life.

# The Beauty Of Nature

A little mommy made her home in our yard. She laid down her three eggs and there she stays. Day after day she sits and waits. Sometime after that her mate came to help her out. He sits with the babies while mommy hunts for food. Every few days we walk down close to the nest to check on the family. We are honored that they chose this space to live. There is so much anticipation waiting for the new arrivals to make their debut. We wait and wait for the day to come. When will it get here? Hurry, hurry please do not be late.

# She Has Been Adopted

My life has been greatly enriched since the day I met her.

She is always there for me anytime I need her. We can talk to

each other about anything and everything. In such a short time

she has become very important to me. I am honored to call her

my best friend but she is so much more than that. She is a

member of my family. My heart and mind have adopted her to

me forever. She has overcome so much in her life and she is a

wonderful person. Any mountain in life she has to climb, she

will always make it to the top and down the other side. She is

the strongest person I know and she has the biggest heart.

There have been times when I have had the feeling of wanting

to curl up in her lap, for she is so comforting and full of love.

All I want is for her to always be happy. I wish her the best

of everything in life. I also hope she always knows how much

I love her. My adopted girl.

# Always So Worried

I know she is grown. It is time to let her go. She has to

make her own way in this big world. I understand this, really

I do. It is just the choices she has made that worry me. She

seems perfectly happy living in an area that is not safe. The

crime is high there. I know all places have their problems.

But why choose a place that is high on the danger list? She

lives with someone who has not had a steady job since she has

known him. They have also moved to and from many homes in a

short time. How can anyone be comfortable without stability?

She is so far away and we can not help if she needs it. We try

so advise her with things we know simply from having lived

longer. Sometimes it feels as if she deliberately chooses

opposite from us for spite. What can a parent do? Nothing

but sit back and take it as is comes. She is grown and on her

own. But the worrying never stops.

# The Place I Call Home

For years I was uncomfortable. Always tense with stress.
Never able to relax. Too much hustle and bustle. Tons of
noise all around. Sirens always going off so loud. Too many
people and too much traffic. No space, no space, never any
space. Never liked it there. Always waiting for a way out.
Then one day everything changed. Things moved at a slower
pace. So much quietness. Space and more space, everywhere
you look. So relaxing with the sounds of nature. Peaceful
and calming. I felt the moment when the stress left my
limbs. No other place could ever make me feel more
comfortable. This is the difference between the big city
and the more rural area of the little city. This is how I knew
I was finally home to stay.

# She Is Missed

She was always so sweet. With fur so soft it felt like silk.

Her shape was long and lean. Her eyes a beautiful shade of gold.

Always so warm she was when she curled up on your lap. She had

a gentleness about her and a wonderful spirit. She had a habit

of sticking her tongue out a bit and putting it against your

shirt when she sat with you. Never did know why she did this.

Just another part of what made her so special. So quick she

was to purr for you and let you know how she felt. She was

a happy baby. Always full of love.

Then one day everything changed. She could barely keep

her eyes open. Always full of gooey crud and crusted

closed. A warm, wet cloth was used to wipe them clean

regularly. Her breathing got harder for her. She could no

longer breath with her mouth closed. She struggled so much.

She got so weak she could no longer jump. Her walking

slowed so much it almost stopped. She no longer ate or drank.

Weaker and weaker she got. She picked one spot and there she stayed. A short time later she was called home to the heavens above. Our baby girl was born with a deadly illness we never knew she had.

# Will We Be The Death Of Ourselves

A long time ago a great man said that the demise of this country will come from within itself rather than an outside source. Is that true or false? Is this the road this country is on? Will we cause our own destruction? First of all, I love this country. I do believe this is a great country. But the truth is we do have some problems. Why is it the rich get richer and the poor get poorer? Why can't things change to help those who need it? There are people without homes. Children without enough to eat. People who need medical help but can not afford doctors. And then we have the justice system. Too many criminals are let back out on the streets. If you deliberately kill someone why should you ever be free again? If a person repeatedly commits crimes, take away their freedom. I am not against guns but there is a problem there. They are too easy for the wrong people to get their hands on, and thus more crimes. Why do we help those who destroy themselves? Why do we help companies who waste their money foolishly? Why does our government do things against us and we the little people have to pay the price for it? Yes I love this country. This is a great country. But changes need to be made. We the people can make this a better place to be. Please do not let us kill ourselves. Let our country live!

# What Judgment Are You Guilty Of

Why do we judge people? What gives us that right? People are all different from one another, is that a crime? We judge with race. We judge with religion. We judge with sexual preference. We judge by looks. We judge by money. When, when, when will it stop? If we were all the same, how boring would this world be? We would then stop being people with minds and all be robots. What gives anyone the right to decide what is right or wrong? Are we not our own person to make our own choices? Who says one way is better than another? We are all people, not machines. Things that are right for some does not automatically make them right for others. Do not judge what you do not know. People are free to be themselves. Do you like to make your own choices? If so, then let others make theirs too. Let people live in the way that is best for themselves. Do not judge me, you do not even know me. I am my own person. My mind is free to make my own choices. I am

not better than you and you are not better than me. Live and

let live.

# Over The Edge

It seems like you have been climbing forever. On and on you go. Higher and higher. Must not stop until you get to the top. The air gets thinner and cooler the higher you go. Your breathing changes and your heart feels differently than it did before the climb. Finally you reach the top and let out a slow deep breath. You can look out all around and see for miles. There is a peacefulness that surrounds you. The only sound you hear is the cool wind as it brushes past your ears. As you stand there staring off into the distance, you feel the tension leave your body. After a few moments, you slowly close your eyes and the only thing you feel is calm. Before you know it, you find yourself leaning forward. More and more you lean farther into the wind. You feel it the moment your feet stop touching anything. The next thing you know, you are soaring into the abyss.

# Let The Fire Burn

You see the building engulfed with flames. You are close enough to the fire that it instantly makes you sweat. All around you people are yelling for help. You hear the sirens and the roar of the engines of the fire trucks. People are screaming and running from the burning building. All this time you stand there mesmerized by the brilliant brightness of the fire. All around you is chaos and yet you are stuck in this same spot. You want to do something. Either to help or to run away. You want to turn away and see something else but your eyes never leave the flames. You feel the flames call to you. They have a hold on your whole being. You start to move closer and closer still. Then you feel the flames lick at your skin and the heat over take you. The fire is too strong. The building is a total loss. You know people are dying in the flames and there is nothing you can do to help. All you hear is their last screams. Death came to their door today. Now it claims you too as you are drawn into the death of the flames.

# What Is The Next Step

The tires let out an ear piercing squeal and you smell the burn of the rubber. You hear the shattering of the glass breaking. The hit was so hard it slams you forward into the airbag. As it goes off, it fills the interior with a fog and it burns the edges of your nose. Your head and neck hurt from the force of being thrown back into the seat. You feel sharp pain in your chest from where the seatbelt grabbed a hold of you. There is pain in your knees from where they hit the dashboard. At the point of impact, the first thing you think is what just happened? You are in a state of confusion. Then you notice a new smell. It is a sweet stickiness. At the same time your eye swells shut as you feel something run down your cheek. It is blood and you are cut, for now you realize how the window got broken. In your foggy state of mind you finally hear the sirens of help on the way to you. As you sit and wait, you wonder how will you recover from this? You look around with your one good eye and you see the

destruction of what once was your car. Without a doubt you

know everything is different now. All you can do is sit back

and let whatever happens happen.

# Yoga With A friend

Ok so you know you should at least do something to stretch out your bones and muscles everyday, in way of exercise. The problem with getting it done is, it is too easy to put it off or to just say you do not feel like bothering with it. And then when it actually does get done, it is like you ask yourself why am I doing this? It is just the same routine day after day. It does not seem any fun and it is too easy to give up.

Ok so here is what can make it so much better. Share this experience with a friend. When someone else is there, you have encouragement to keep going. It is something to look forward to instead of dreading. It can also be a great source for laughter, seeing each other in the many poses. Some things are meant to be shared and are so much better when you do.

# To See Her In Pain

You see her agony and discomfort and it tears at your heart.

As you wipe away her tears with your fingers, you know

something needs to be done to make it better. Do something,

do something, hurry, hurry make her pain go away. But what

can you do? It is out of your hands. So you sit and wait. Then

wait some more. All you want to do is make everything alright,

but you can not do that. It is a terrible feeling to have no

control and to feel useless. All you can do is hope that it

will not last long, although it seems too long already. Please,

please make it stop. Take the misery I see from her eyes.

When will I see those beautiful eyes sparkle again?

# Does It Really Matter

Ok, so you both have a different opinion. So what, it is

allowed. No where is it written that everyone has to agree

on every single subject. It is how you react and the things you

do because of it that matters. When a difference occurs you

can go on and stress your point at all costs. Not stopping until

the two of you are angry and ready for a fight. Or another

way to handle it is by stepping back a moment and asking

yourself does it really matter? Is it life changing? Will the

sun stop rising? Will the grass stop growing? Will your daily

lives change in any way or will things still go on as they always

have? If nothing will be different just because of having two

opinions between you then maybe the best thing to do is tell

yourself it does not matter. You are both your own person.

It does not make one right and one wrong. All it means is

you both have a mind and you are using it with your own

free will. We are people, not clones. Let the small stuff go.

# Make The Pain Stop

Pain, pain all you feel is pain. From you head down to your toes and everywhere in between. Everything hurts and you do not know why. Day after day you try not to move anymore than absolutely necessarily. What is wrong? No idea at all. You feel like you want to rip your insides out just to make it stop. But you know you can not and will not do that. It feels like your head will explode at any moment. You wish it would just so you do not hurt anymore. But you know that will never happen. So what do you do? There is no cure. All you know is it is slowly killing you. Little by little. Piece by piece. You wait for the end to come. How long will it take? No one knows. Day after day you wait for someone or something to make the pain stop.

# Is This The Day You Die

You are walking down the street. Just taking a walk. Not really going anywhere, just stretching the bones. Then out of nowhere someone walks up to you. They point a gun at you and you freeze to the spot you are standing in. While still aiming the gun in your direction, they slowly circle around you. Your fear keeps you from speaking. But your mind is screaming. What is the reason for this? What does this person want? They stop their movements and stand beside you. The gun is aimed at your head. Softly they whisper to you is this the day you die? You do not answer. Your eyes close in fear of what will come next. You then hear a loud click next to your ear. The person says this is not your day. You are still frozen to your spot. By the time your eyes open, you are all alone. With your heart pounding in your chest, you run for home. Thankful to be alive.

# Gone But Not Forgotten

He was a good brother. He was a great husband. He was a wonderful man. His body was not young anymore. He had his share of health issues. But they were under control. His mind, as always, was sharp as a tack. Never missing a moment. Then suddenly it happens. His heart gives out and he never makes it through the night. Why? Why did he have to go? Why did he leave? It hurts to know he is gone. But your love for him never lessens. He is missed. He is your uncle. Your favorite uncle. But you never had the chance to tell him how much he means to you and how much you love him. You hope now he knows your thoughts. Rest in peace uncle. Rest in peace. For one day we will see each other again.

# And So It Goes

Day after day, week after week. So much pain that will not go away. Feeling so weak. Energy almost not even there. Doing the littlest thing can wear you out. Stand too long and the light headedness comes. Everything hurts so much you want to rip your insides out. You go to see a doctor and they have no clue what the problem is. Wait a few more days and then see a different doctor. Still the same answer. No idea what is wrong. So you wait and wait some more. Soon you will go to another doctor. Do you even dare to hope that the problem will be solved? Will the mystery of what is wrong then be revealed? Or will the same things continue? Will you ever get your normal life back? Or are you doomed to be forever plagued by illness?

# Just To Drive

Your day is clear, with nothing planned to do. The sun is shining and it is beautiful outside. So what do you do with all this time that has been presented to you? Grab your keys and head out the door. Into your car and away you go. Find some back roads where there is not very much traffic. Just pick a direction and drive. Open the windows and feel the air wash across your skin and through your hair. Feel the warmth of the sun. Notice as much as you can as you pass by. Maybe there will be something rare to see. Or maybe things you have not seen in a long time. Come to a cross road and pick a different direction. Have no particular destination in mind to reach. Leave all your worries behind. Just enjoy the day and your mini getaway.

# Our Country's Hero

The images and memories will forever be in his mind. He has gone through his own personal hell from what he has seen. He knows first hand how it feels to be in the situation of kill or be killed. He has fought for this country. He has been face to face with our enemies. He is one of many who have fought for the freedom we all take for granted. Without people like him, our country would not exist. He is a hero for putting his life on the line for the rest of us. Do not judge him or his sacrifices until you have walked in his shoes. If people like him do not stand up for this country, then who will? And what will become of us? War is hell for everyone, but sometimes it is necessary to remain free. Honor those who have put their lives in the line of fire for us. Without them this country will be no more.

# Are Birds Crazy

So you are driving in your car. Down the street you go. Not
a lot of traffic as you drive. Birds fly by here and there. But
what catches you by surprise is what the birds do. Do they
like to be daring? Do they like to risk their lives? They fly so
close to your car that you barely miss hitting them. Sometimes
they pass right by your windshield so close that it makes you
jump. Other times they fly in front of your car and you could
swear that you must have hit them because you do not see
them come out past the other side. Where did they go? Did
they just disappear? You stop and check the front of your
car. Not a single feather do you see. No marks from a bird
on your car. No trail of birds left behind in the road. Why
do they fly like this? Are birds crazy? Or are they just
entertaining you?

# Pain In His Head

His head hurts. More than a normal headache. This pain is severe. Pounding, throbbing pain. Make it stop, it hurts too much. Out of the blue, he suddenly drops to the floor. He has blacked out, unaware of how scared you are to see him this way. All you can do is sit beside him and wait for him to come out of it. Why is this happening? Make it go away. You can do nothing. This can happen again at any time. If he is ever hit in the head, it could be the death of him. You worry about him every day. You want to protect him and keep him safe. It is out of your control. There is a time bomb in his head. You pray that it never goes off. Do not let this tumor be the death of him. Let him live a full life with many years to come.

# The Miracle Of Life

Life was created deep inside. Your body goes through so many changes. Day after day. Week after week. Month after month. Growing bigger and bigger all the time. Developing into a little person who you already love so much and can not wait to meet. Anticipation grows along with this life. It is amazing what the body is capable of making. To know you have the power to create life is the ultimate feeling a person can have. Truly a miracle from a higher power. You will mold and shape this one's mind and heart. So many things they eagerly await to learn from you. It is a wonderful feeling but it can also be overwhelming to have their fate in your hands. So many experiences and challenges are brought to you with this new life. Do not be afraid of them. Embrace them all. They will all make you a better and stronger person.

# His Eyes Say It

He was happy. Lots of smiles and everything was fine. Make some memories was said. Something to look back on in years to come. This is something good. Something he will want to remember. Then I watched the change wash over his face. The happiness left his eyes and was replaced with a coldness. He was mad. Pushed too far. He was not in control and he did not like it. He compared the past to the here and now. They are clearly not the same. He was showed a different point of view, but he felt as if he was being shoved. It hurt to see him that way. To see that look in his eyes. A line was crossed. Things were said that maybe should not have. It went too far. Someone put their two cents in when they should have kept quiet. I hope I never see his eyes look like that again.

# Expressions In Sleep

A baby's face in sleep holds many wonders. Sometimes there are lines in the forehead. Other times there are not. The brows move up and down. One at a time or both together. The eyes pinch tight or relax. You can see them move behind the lids. Back and forth or fluttering about. Sometimes the nose wrinkles up. Other times it is smooth. The mouth twitches in every direction. The lips purse as in the blow a kiss. Then the lip raises in a sneer. Next you see a smile. Soon you see a sad face in a silent cry. At last the face brightens as if with a laugh. So many expressions in one small place.

# Late Night Run

So it has been a long, hard day. Coming and going here and there, racing all about. You finally make it home, glad the day is over. You try to relax, but you can not sit still. The energy is flowing through you like a raging river. You decide to go for a run in the night air. So off you go, out the door and down to the street. You run for a few blocks, trying to clear your mind. Block after block, you keep running. It feels good to breath in the night air. Slowly the stress from the day leaves you. You begin to relax and enjoy the run.

Suddenly you hear a car coming from behind you. You do not think too much about it because every now and then cars have driven by while you have been running. Then you hear the car get closer and it slows down. Someone calls from the window and asks if you want a ride. You reply with a no and keep running. So you run for another block or so and the same car shows up next to you again. The people inside still want you to accept a ride from them. You say a forceful no and run faster.

The car keeps following you. You start to cut through yards and

go onto different streets. Still you hear the car chasing after

you. At the end of a street, the car stops in front of you and

blocks your path. They open a door and yell for you to get in.

You scream no at them and dash through the closest yard.

Yard after yard, street after street, you hear the car

coming after you. There is no escape from this menacing

presence. You can not outrun it, so you decide you must hide.

So you sneak through a few yards, looking for some place

you will be safe. Then you find a spot. It is a small place with no

lighting. You curl up into a tight little ball and figure no one will

see you. Slowly time passes by and you start to hurt from your

bones being cramped up. By now you are tired and want to

sleep. You squeeze your eyes shut tight and wish this to all be

over. You start to hear sounds around you and they are getting

closer. You send up a little prayer of help, then take a deep

breath and hold it. Hoping you will not be discovered.

Everything around you goes silent. You let out your breath

and open your eyes. You then look straight into the face of evil.

You let out a scream and bolt upright into a sitting position. You

take a couple breaths and look around. You are home and in your

bed. Then you realize…it was all a dream.

# To Bleed

The floor is cold, hard tile. Unyielding with your weight upon

it. You slowly slide down the wall until you are sitting flat on your

bottom. You wear nothing and soon the coldness seeps into your

warm flesh until you no longer notice. You stare off in a daze at

the tile that surrounds you. Suddenly the light glints off of the

object you hold between your fingers. Your eyes move and focus

on it. It is small and shiny, with a sharp edge. After staring at it

for a few moments, you know what you must do. Very slowly, you

take the blade across your skin. You feel the tug as it rips

apart. As you are doing this, you watch the blood sprout up

from the cut. You are soon numb to any pain this has caused you.

It mesmerizes you as you watch the blood flow from the wound

like a tiny river. It pools on the floor and follows the paths

between the tiles. You watch your life supply as it drains from

your flesh. Soon your eyes want to close and your head becomes

heavy. You lean over until your head is on the floor. As you stare at the mess you made, your eyes slowly close. The last thought

you have is wondering if someone will find you? Or will you

forever sleep?

# Silently Screaming

You sit in a room full of darkness. No light, no sound. No one is there with you. You look calm and relaxed on the outside. You silently scream at all the madness on the inside. No one can hear you. No one can help you. Then it happens, suddenly there is another sound. You hear all of the whispers in the dark. So many coming at you all at once. They expect you to have all of the right answers. What can you do? What can you say? No where to run. No place to get away. Make it stop! Make it stop! Make it all go away. You want to hide, but you can not escape. So you silently scream some more. Then take a deep calming breath and tackle the questions head on until they all have the answers they seek. You do the best you can, not always getting it right. Daily life is full of questions. Many times it can be overwhelming. Sometimes the only release you have is to silently scream.